As an Australian woman, born and raised on Aboriginal and Torres Strait Islander land, I would like to acknowledge the Traditional Owners and Custodians of the land on which I stand, and pay my respects to Elders past and present.

I would like to raise awareness to the assimilation of our First Nations people.

And I would like to *celebrate* you.

I am a product of my environment. The air in my lungs, the water in my brain, – all comes from Noongar Country. I am grateful for the Whadjuk and Bindjareb people, of the Noongar nation, who have graciously shared their beautiful home with me for all of my 23 years.

To Aboriginal and Torres Straight Islander peoples all over, I am blessed to be by your side, standing on your grounds. I am in love with your Connection to Country, and I am so grateful to you for taking such good care of Our Home.

I understand what a blessing *and privilege it is* to be on Blak country. Without your pain I wouldn't know joy. I see you as our original storytellers of the Earth. I appreciate that if not for your Dreamtime, or Rainbow Serpent, I would not have a place to call home. *Not a story to tell.* I respect that I would not be here today, or have any of the luxuries I do, if you had not come before me. If you had not endured *all you have.*

I stand here with you, and I am eternally grateful. It always was, and it always will be, Aboriginal Land.

I have attached a link to the HealingFoundation.

A national organisation partnering with communities, to address the ongoing trauma caused by Australia's colonisation, that Aboriginal and Torres Straight Islander people still face in 2025. An appalling tragedy. I ask you to please educate yourselves on this matter, and simply donate as you can.

https://healingfoundation.org.au/?form=fungzechuud

Everything is Already Hell

Olive Tostevin

ISBN: 978-1-7638500-8-8

Cover Design by Anze Ban Virant, ABV Atelier Design
Interior Formatting by Furkan Süperdoğan

If you or someone you know
is experiencing suicidal thoughts or struggling
with mental illness in any capacity, help is available.
Don't wait until it's too late,
get treatment - *men* and women.
I tell you well informed by my own experience -
you *can* feel better, but it is you who is to do the work.
Make a doctor's appointment
what have you got to lose?

I am getting out all the bad art, so I can start making good art.

Contents

Prologue

thought my home growing up was
as big as a universe,
thought mums and dads chose
the weather every day
thought *your abuse* just,
the necessary part of a household -
i couldn't have known differently
with his layers of angry red.

while you're reaching the age
we begin forming opinions,
interpreting social cues
it is sunshine and rainbows
we just have different versions
of that rainbow
we can't seem to agree on,
who makes the sun shine.

you torched my life
in every way
you have given me
the weightiest complex.
everything
has you written all over
i will fight this to death,
your nothingness will
continue to exist
while i stand here, with my accolades.
my mere existence proof
i have already won.

i already did the
amazing things
anything after this,
my retirement.

the drive from my house to yours,
merely five minutes long
i was only two streets
away from my own.
ouch my head
what the hell
just happened

i told you i'd had
a car accident
you asked are you still coming
i answered, *yes.*

when did I become
this silly girl?

temazepam
aripiprazole
olanzapine
sertraline
mianserin
risperidone

doing my head in
yet i am still.
be my true self
manage my behaviour
or just escape
turn into a shell?

i've been in this battle
a while now
i don't even know
i care to be fighting

- six prescriptions in twelve months

i need to get out of this hell
i call hometown
every corner laced with memories,
i wish i would forget -
death. heartbreak. embarrassment. neglect.
even when i close my eyes
i still see it all
my mind tortures my mind
all day, *everyday*
until it doesn't -
instead silence.
i don't have thoughts or feelings
i just lay in bed,
a difficult way to live
between a rock and my self.

i need to get out of my head

-

i am back in the hospital
i don't know what to say
i am trying to write
how i feel about it all.
nothing has come
i feel nothing
or i am choosing to feel
some version of nothing.
any alternative,
too awful to bear
He's a great distraction -
until i focus on focusing.
my underlying constant
i just want to die

2024

i won't put on a jumper this morning
my nervous tummy
has the goose flesh on my arms
to distract from the cold
my stomach has fallen
to the floor
feels so *squishy,*
no fast beating heart
thats how
i can tell it apart
not anxiety but butterflies
i'm just thinking of you.
i think i just want
to close my eyes
on your chest
i think i might feel
so safe finally.
i'm so scared to try,

i have failed everything so far -
how wasteful i would be
to fail *you* my dear.

when i write,
it could feel like
i am looking at someone else.
it is like
i am watching a film
i look down
and there're words on the paper.

it's always felt so personal,
i'm so scared to write of you
never offered this away before
you feel more personal
than my writing ever has,
it wouldn't make sense
to keep us apart.

- letting myself let you in

you are sweet
to think *i am great*
i feel so loved by you,
you hardly know me.
i have been waiting for you
i would always wait again
you make me feel allowed
to take up space in the world
you have me thinking
men
aren't all that scary.
i feel so myself by you.

- *a better version of me*

i have no words
to explain this thing
besides simply
they call him fish.
so spoilt to find
the human i did
who has given
such clarity
such sanctuary to me.
all the things
i will ever need
to be all the people
i am supposed to be.

whether forever
or not long enough,
simply knowing this love
is so completely
enough.
all i'll ever need,

in this little life.
getting to hold this love
every day
truly just,
a miracle.

i am here to absorb
the culture
defend my women,
and buy my flowers.
i could eat my lemons,
grow her heart
love, this boy
and everything else.
on this wondrous day -
i feel abundant.

i swore i wasn't gay
i swore i wasn't straight either
something you do
    does something to me.
am i lying to myself
or telling you the truth?
all that seems to matter
getting to lie next to you.
anything else,
i'd just call noise.

one percent

how unlikely to find
my spare parts walking around
on another side of the country,
we will always meet
in every life.
take the chance of us here,
as proof
my love.
you are it
you're all of it
now and forever,
    if you'll have me.

crack

a human living everyday
so many emotions,
so many feelings.
being loved exactly
for who i am,
somehow blinding me
to all before.

i was so depressed
so continuously anxious,
i didn't see how bad
things *really were.*
my relief in those times
my feeling better
a basement of sad
a miserable grey,
it's all gone now
i can't explain it.

i still get anxiety
and i still feel sad
but it's normal now
and it's *because of him.*

there will be hard times forever,
the quicker i learn to accept them
the better they can be.
every second of life so enjoyable,
so existent in anything.

my love as an example;
when he is not himself
still somehow *he soothes*
every piece of my broken heart.
he allows me to feel *good*
on a higher level.
it's *unbelievable*
to be completely clear -
i can touch this love
look across the room
and watch the hurt, melt away.
this love of yours
    my new favourite drug.

i don't feel
like a poet
what am i doing here
i
feel so existential

you are writing
aren't you?

olive tostevin

i don't know
if the way i'm feeling
is valid
or not
i still feel hurt
thinking back on it
a day and some later
all i can say, *i need better.*

to be the person
pointing at your flaws,
is almost as painful
as they themselves.
you know
just how perfect
i think you are

no one is looking out for me
if i don't do it myself
i cannot let these prickles
continue to root
i must tell you directly -
they hurt my poor feet

i always revert back
to making myself small
i am important as anyone else
i am acceptable as i am.
what am i doing here
why do i feel like this
am i sad because
i ran out of medication
pms
or real sad?
who's taking care of me
when i'm taking care of him?
lately, it all seems
to hurt *just the same.*

why do i keep doing this?
alone in a crowded city
at nine in the afternoon again
grounding myself in a mcdonalds
i'm stepping in for the first time
as i try to find my way to a swimming pool
i have no clue how to get to
phone in hand dying
with the directions i need
to keep moving backwards.
bought an uber here
after i lost myself on a bus
going the wrong way
my boyfriend is somewhere
drunk in the city. i don't know where
because i don't know who i am
anymore. i just want to go home
to a place i'm not really welcome

but pay to rent anyway
choices to end up
basically nowhere
feeling like i'm everywhere,
all at once.
i tell my hometown friends
things are amazing
just a fancy way of saying
i'm not doing so well.
whenever i run away
i stop to catch my breath
i'm afraid if i wait too long
i'll miss the next bus.

- this feels diagnosable just not today

it feels like i'm trying hard
to be what you need
as many different versions of myself
to match how you feel
happy
excited
obsessively stressed
there will never be a version
to match careless and unthoughtful
it is really quite simple,
i deserve as i give.

i am caring
to myself
my love,
and my family.
i care about
and for him
i care,
i am caring.

~~why don't i~~
~~care?~~

a tragedy

do not confuse this with feminine rage
it is simply justice.
i wish it didn't have to happen this way
i know i deserve better.
if it were someone else
they may not have gone to the police
they may not have been bruised enough to know
we are not supposed to just take it
we are supposed to make noise.
men cannot go around torturing us for fun
and see no punishment
meet no consequence
they shall take responsibility.
a man sexually assaulted me in broad daylight
in a public space
in the middle of the day.

where the fuck do you suppose
   i am to feel safe in my own skin?

i will not settle with traumatised
belittled or disrespected
i will speak up for as long as i can
as loud as i must

as apparently my voice
   is the only luxury i possess

as a woman living
   in your cruel world.

not only did you
rob me of my safety
but thanks to your fuck face
i lost
my favourite jumper as well
they needed to take it as evidence
i hope you go to hell
and come back a better man.

i do not want to scratch my face open
with my overgrown fingernails
that was just an intrusive thought.
the world will not end
because he left the lid off his pen.
it feels like i don't
know anything but this.

oh dear
it's getting bad again
the *oh this is never going to go away*
pain is back
he took it away for a while this time

olive tostevin

i've been reading a lot lately
self help mostly
i never thought that'd be me,
never interested me before
i used to read romance
i can't think of anything worse
the books i read
felt so out of reach
so unrealistic
not something meant for me
now that i have it,
i read self help
i'm wondering if there's a number
of books i can read,
that will lead to me
finding
the answers i seek

can we sleep on the phone?

i didn't want you to leave
i don't know why
you stayed to begin with
how did i do this
for so many years?
so silently unbearable
as in i haven't said a word
in two whole days,
without you here
to wish a good morning
i simply have
no reason to speak.

- *vacation*

why do i feel like this
one hundred times a day?
it's getting so hard
everyday
it should be so good
i have everything i wanted
i feel awful.
my fish died last night
i have a bad feeling.
don't let this mean anything
you are just superstitious.

touch wood
my brain demanded -
i have the goofy kind.
the sad makes sense
the anxious too
be happy - drugs, drink, *cry.*
you feel anxious, you panic
sweat, squirm.
the obsessive one makes me
pick up my crumbs?
put my keys on a hook?
organise my wardrobe
to the pattern of a rainbow?
i can't enjoy getting dressed
to go out on my date
i can't remember what went where
why i wanted it there in the first place.

does it sound goofy
does it sound *rational?*
these days i find
i don't have much else left

- *obsessive compulsive disorder*

i just want a quick fix
when i get that painful feeling
instant relief
i need to slow down.
point towards something
i care about
something i want.
when i try i'm good at it
i don't want to oftentimes.
i always want to get, really really high
it's so easy
and i can get very *lazy*

my room smells like weed all the time
i don't want in my head
do i even like it these days?

i'm sorry again.

i feel so,
consumably sad
i thought he made it
go away
i knew deep down
that was all a ploy
it does go away -
until he does too
how selfish i'd be
to ask him to stay,
whatever would i do
should he truly leave?

oh god
i am such a hoarder
i haven't thrown anything
out in years.
i still have this little voice
telling me i deserved it,
so used and dirty,
and so close to my chest.
it's probably been
rubbing off on me *by now.*
oh god what if someone
can smell it across the room?
what if it's on my clothes *or*
influencing how i choose men?

crumble

olive tostevin

everything is already hell

olive tostevin

everything is already hell

how could this happen again?
everything looks like you

everything is already hell

olive tostevin

everything is already hell

olive tostevin

everything is already hell

olive tostevin

i can feel the depression spreading
so tired before it even started
i am still catching up
on weeks of missed sleep.
how am i to fight this
again and again
my charge already so low
capacity for great,
already so small
i've simply no room
  for awfully sad.

everything is changing so fast,
~~*i thought he was depressed.*~~

everything is already hell

olive tostevin

i never wrote about you like this.
it never felt this bad with you.

everything is already hell

olive tostevin

we accidentally
call each other baby.
i wouldn't hug
someone else like you.

we're just friends.
we're just friends.

everything is already hell

everything
i ever wanted
what happened to my
princess castle
you light it up
with every tantrum,
each curse erasing
a memory shared
please stop and remember
who this is
i don't want to think
of you like this

- i don't want it to end this way

what's going on?
you're scaring me dear.
please come home
it's not safe out there.
i'm clutching my heart
i'm thinking the worst,
if you can bring yourself home -
    i could keep you safe.

i can't seem to help myself,
a poet after all.
just as the man in his kitchen
can't help but yell
as he drops a fork.
a perfect match -
you learned to blame the ocean,
an alcoholic's daughter
will never
throw in the towel.
you lost yourself
in waves of emotion,
i watched as my butterflies,
slowly drowned.
yours was the hand, i asked to hold at their wake.

- how could i blame him, we were only learning to swim

friends with benefits?

i am obsessed
i am over you
i am under you again
i won't know how
to disappear from you
why would i need to
i am itching inside
away from you
i am lighting a fire
to attract you moth,
you are more of a fish
you won't ever,
take my bait.

i must've done something wrong
but you said *forever*
i can get through hard things
i can't understand your logic,
i was telling the truth;
i still think you're wonderful.

break

your name is everywhere i look,
i live by the ocean
i've felt like a fish
my entire life.

i can't stop thinking,
about your warmth
holding your hand
driving one hundred,
listening to you
listening to sam fender,
i want to be warm again -
you made everything
so warm.

thinking about
his hands on my body
looking back too much
never getting things done
it's already happened
think about whats to come -
as long as i look forward
    i can't make a wrong turn.

- write the book

"i will never drink alcohol, so as not to turn out like
     my father."
now he is dead, and i am a recovering alcoholic.
keep seeing ads for this pain every place i go. the
     train station plastering it on the staircase, my
     complimentary water served
in an empty vodka bottle - my drink of choice for a
     while, vanilla with the lid off
we aren't allowed smoking commercials anymore,
     but should you wish to drink yourself to death,
     a trivia night and, we're asked to figure out the
     liquor behind a blurred label?
i'm in the minority i know
but *God* where does it end. while you get to
     swallow your pinot noirs, i'm swallowing my
     words to make you all comfortable.

swallowing pills like temazepam and
"they did the best they could with the information
    they were given."
they make us take a test to get a licence, *but any
    idiot can raise a kid.*
consider myself lucky i got sober enough *to want* to
    get sober again.
was it my genetic predisposition, or the exposure
    of hearing yes when i was 8 and asked for
    another sip?
my favourites became whisky and beers, just like
    you dad -
thank you for showing me; *you couldn't be trusted.*

psychosis

i know whats going on. i am blind in my thoughts.
to reality. what is reality to me delusion and worries
my family. i don't care what you think. i hate you
when i'm here. in my rational mind it's simply
you are not here. i want to be where you are. i am
clawing my way out. of a hole that isn't getting
deeper but wider. i watch my favourite television to
ground to a moment. this reminder of reality makes
it seem possible to get back. i'm impatient i know
all the answers. i don't want to rest and shower
and eat. i want better. right now, please. so tired
but i can't sleep. broken but i will not stop. i know
psychosis and me is just getting through. sometimes
in hospital. once for a month. an involuntary hold.
a high i've never craved more. i fear it when i'm
not here. only when i'm inside do i love it. i want to
eat it for breakfast and dessert. it tastes like drugs
without them. i want to smoke so badly my brain
says. walk into a different hole. i want to slice my
wrists open when i'm here in sweet psychosis. on
weed i just want off weed. an easier hole. psychosis
is impossibility to choose life. it is unfathomable to
see anything but an end.

it's like poison and candy at once
so sickly

but it tastes so good
i have been struggling to eat these last few weeks
i can't be bothered
i know i am melting away.
such a struggle
to put clothes on
to get in the car
if i go to the store
i can eat well
i arrive home
with eighteen cans of tuna
three steaks
a kilogram of yoghurt
one of cheese
two litres of milk
a ham and cheese bread
two different types of chocolate
i've been a vegan for seven years

in this fracture of reality
nothing matters but survival
when my mind goes under
it somehow remembers
to stock up on supplies
while we hide out in the bunker
she knows we lose capacity
to wait for things to cook

or to get out of bed
she grabs quick and easy
calorie dense
high in nutritional value.
i asked for the chocolate
in case she decides
i deserve a treat
now i have a stocked cupboard
and eighteen choices
of do i slit my throat
or just go back to bed

it feels like
an evil spirit
i need to exterminate
i've never been good at killing spiders.

i know this isn't good for me
when i'm sick like this
it feels like a requisite
if you want to be a poet
what if i can't write
when i feel okay
i won't think like that
far more painful than

whats happening now
when i break into these
depths of insanity
i feel powerful and righteous
anything conceivable
when the world is in fragments
i want to be a writer
god help me.

when does this end?
faith in gods plan
he must have a vision
i feel blind
he must have a vision
i cannot see

praise god
thy will be done
over and over in my mind
until i get back
he has the answers
i can't feel right now
i know he will
show me the way
how could i deny his existence

i've felt delusion
i know there is light
i will see you again

i've got this under control
thinking i've got it under wraps
so i go to the doctor
just to get back on my medicine
she's throwing around words
like schizophrenia and
are you going to take yourself to hospital again
i thought i was just stressed
i thought i was healing from a breakup
i have been here since 16
since you died
you got what i always wanted
i think i hated you for that
all i remember thinking about
since i was a little girl
how miserable life is
i wanna grow up
to learn how to kill myself
i'm too little to know whats good for killing
i will figure out a way when i am grown
the voices have been like this forever
i swear to god i thought it was just like that

i thought everything happened this way
for everyone

who's in here
it isn't me
someone else
is eating me alive
something else
is steering my ship

god
i can't stop eating again
i already healed this i thought.
i already fixed this issue i said
no no
it's the issue of
you are not enough that is making you eat
you are not an eating disorder or a drug addict
you are just a person with a hole
how you wish to fill it is up to you
god
how could you say that
after all we've been through
i don't want to decide for myself
anymore

just tell me the way
i trust you isn't that enough?
i don't want to be the author
any longer
just show me what to do
and i'll do it
i promise

these drugs are so strange
i know how to smoke
myself to sleep
i know how to drink
until i wake on the bathroom floor
how do i stay interested
on this antidepressant
how do i not just
turn the world off
it's so silent on this drug
is anybody even here

i can't feel much
of anything
these days
so i write to myself
i say it all here
i have no one to talk to
if i don't know this pencil

everything is already hell

olive tostevin

everything is already hell

olive tostevin

i've been reading again
cycle tracking, periods.
my best friend sent a book
this birthday just past
it's teaching me how
to utilise each phase
i am due in a few days
excited to bleed.
i am writing down physical,
emotional symptoms
gearing up for
my most knowledgable winter.

now the time has come and gone
without a single drop of blood
i am in such a bad spot
she didn't come this month
with all this new information
i know exactly what i've done
i've hurt myself too much
my body doesn't think we're safe.
she wouldn't release an egg this month
she knows me far too well,
knows if we got pregnant
i couldn't take care of our little baby.
how could you do this to us?

- *i don't want to be like you anymore*

what if it's just like this for me
how do i find the value in sticking around
how do i muster the energy to go have a shower
please can you just brush my teeth?

olive tostevin

all we did today
walk from the bed
to the food
to the bathroom,
i feel blue

she says life feels like this for her sometimes
she says it hasn't been this bad for years.
i can't believe
what we see in the mirror
i can't believe, she let it go this far.
she's tearing apart
at the seams again
i'm over it,
i've caught my *own disease.*

some days, when i
look in the mirror
i don't recognise
who's staring back,
don't remember making choices
to get me *this thin*
i might pick up the phone
and fall to pieces, i'm not strong enough
to hold the weight
not ready to hear myself
say i'm not doing well,
i'm not interested
in texting you back.
my silence means -
i'm unhappy again

under the covers,
waiting to come out.
hasn't been this way
in awhile i,
will relearn how
to tell myself no,
i can remember i have
a family,
i remind myself i
really wouldn't
want my sister
to lose her sister.
i will live however long, *she does.*

- *why aren't the antidepressants doing their job?*

i don't remember
who i am anymore
my head a mirror
to whoever is looking.
i will tell you what
you want to hear
i wish to tell the truth
and do it well
i wish to run around
like a kid in the street
stumbling if i must,
rising as quick as she can.
i don't remember how
good feels anymore
i am falling asleep
to my own life again.

i don't want to look at the beaches he swam in
my father died in this town,
that's enough of a reason.

my emotions i feel
disconnected from,
mood fluctuations
will come back
she said.
i can't find the motivation
i'm depressed yes
i know for that
i can give myself slack.
i don't know what to do
which path to follow
just be here
now
thats enough
stick around,
don't pressurise everything

- it will figure a way out.

i just want my eyes to close
but *i have to close them*
on this new drug
they are so open
when everything else
is so ready for bed
i wish someone were here
to tuck me in.

bleeding again

i'm daydreaming about
the outline of your toes
i'm thinking of you,
for something to do.
i like the shape of your fingers,
the veins in your arms
i remember you hating
how skinny you'd gotten
i always thought
you looked *beautiful,*
the way your brown hair parted
after you let me cut it -
i adored being in love with you
i drink decaf now
i don't smoke anymore
still i like to feel woozy,
so this time it's you
in your pair of black jeans,

your white t-shirt
and the memory of us,
it's pancakes for dinner
when we left before paying.

i'm trying to stay sane,
so i put you in my mind
after everything, you're still
my new favourite drug.

off balance

always glad it happened,
it just doesn't seem fair
a libra i am
only my nature to share.
not mad at you for
being done with the ride,
you just shouldn't have jumped off,
while I was high.

- you broke up with me over a bong

i am thankful for the grass
i am thankful for the sun
i am thankful for a brain
that won't give up.

slow down,
pay attention.
your body knows
what she's talking about.

i am trying to multitask
trying to mourn my relationship,
be his friend, and heal at once
it's very tricky
i'm a terrible juggler.
you are learning something new
be gentle with yourself
and with him
you are gentle to your friends.

i've never met anyone like you
thats a good thing
stop hurting yourself,
you're okay on your own
no ones coming to save you

- we've learnt this before

what this teaches me
the importance of acceptance
and letting go.
i don't have a father
i'm not in a relationship,
my baseline is low
i can't change any of that
i need to live anyway
i know this in theory,
i just struggle with action.

the colour in my cheeks
is coming back,
i like the way my teeth look in the mirror.
my therapist told me
start dating again
i've been holding off in hopes,
you might come back.
how foolish i was,
how painful it's been -
i heard my mind saying,
i wanted you to.

what am i afraid of?
him she says
i am telling myself
i am *afraid* of him.
i am not -
afraid only of
rejection
humiliation, embarrassment, hurt.
none of those are now
stuck in *victim brain*
i will feel these things
about myself
should i listen to the anxiety,
give in to the stress.
i feel nervous i don't
feel safe with attention,
he's going to give me his attention.
it seems so frightening,
i know it's healthy.

i can notice my anxiety
and also not be
utterly and completely
consumed by it.
this really is
an exciting revelation.

suddenly anything
feels attainable
every second spent with you
feels like a gift,
given on purpose.
not to teach me magic and
~~disappear~~ as your final act,
but to show me it's out there
to teach me *what i can do.*

i will never not think,
you are a beautiful man.

you were never put here to hurt me
you were just trying your best
it's no one's fault, mine was bigger than yours
i can hold the weight of that
if it's not goodbye forever
you became my best friend -
before and after.
why should i lose you
because you fell in love,
with the wrong girl?

i know everything about you
and *for what,* now
i don't give up this easy,
i'll worry about you -
finding a nice lady
i know who you deserve
i would never want to see,
to hear you've settled
you're worth more than you think,
good luck out there

i found vital nourishment
in seasonal fruits,
handpicked for me
by my female farmers.
while i slurped up the juice,
i got a taste for the sweet
so i kept all the seeds
for my very own garden.
now we eat fruit
no matter the season,
each basket abundant
as we sow for our sisters.

how did it come to this
how am i to love a man
music straight to his ears
as we stroll the beach
no reason to say hello
to the lady walking by.
i want him to woo me
need the scent of my perfume
he wouldn't even smell it
busy with his many princesses.

- *on a screen*

i don't have much sense
of a home when i go
i don't really know
that i have it at all.
i've always hoped to be someplace else
i thought i would be stuck
right here forever
i'd just like to go
where the wind wants me,
no particular sense of self
around other people.
like a clown following a circus
making friends as he goes,
just happy to be there
getting the people to laugh.

now it's all making sense
all hurting much less
not my husband
or baby's father
but a guy,
who got me out.
showed me there's more
than one rainbow,
i liked yours
(i liked you.)

Epilogue

i am walking myself home again
this time i will just smell the flowers
finally i admit, they were never mine to pick.
the pain has come in
the love back where it belongs.
never a silly girl, i am a *kind woman*
you couldn't begin to fathom,
what we contain.
my period has come back
and everything is already hell.

i fuckin hate you man, and your birthday is tattooed on my wrist

i remember you ripping my shirt off outside my kindergarten classroom because i had it on inside out. you noticed the moment i was about to walk into class, instead of before i left the house, because you never even looked at me. i remember you whisper screaming through angry gritted teeth at Emily's hockey game, when i dropped the tub of chips too big for my little hands. i remember playing barbies and pretending my ken was a good man in a happy marriage, and the yelling we heard through the dollhouse walls was just the neighbour who didn't know how to love right. i remember you making my mother cry and yell more often than not. i remember going vegetarian again after you moved out, because you forced me into eating meat while i was 'being too difficult.' you made every hard thing ten times

worse. you stood on my neck while i was learning
to breathe. you taught me *children should be seen,
and not heard.* you took every good thing i ever
had and made it feel dangerous. i'm not sad that
you're gone. all it means for me now is the freedom
to be whoever i want, to do whatever i choose
to. without the fear you put in me since the day i
started speaking. now i can say whatever i feel. any
fear i have of what someone may think of my art
is nothing in comparison to the fear i had just from
being your daughter. happy birthday asshole, i hope
you're regretting every word you ever said to me.
god and i have been on great terms for a while now,
i'd be worried where your next beer is coming from
if i were you.

for some reason when you died i threw on a pair of
rose coloured glasses. i turned every horrible thing
you did into i miss you and i wish you were still

here. the fact of the matter is we hardly knew each
other. you talked to me like a piece of dirt on the
bottom of your shoe, and i didn't talk to you *at all*.
i hid in my room when i heard you enter the house.
i pretended you weren't there when you drove me
to school. i hated you all the way up until i didn't,
and only when you died did i realise what i'd been
missing all those years. a father who protected me
from the scary and mean of the world. instead you
brought it to the dinner table - you made eating
meals feel like a military operation, of *sit down
shut up and don't leave the table until your bowl is
empty.* i read the back of the cereal box over and
over to drown out the thoughts of i wish you were
dead, that started swirling around in grade three. i
learned then just how powerful my mind is; though
i've read the nutritional value of a weetbix everyday
for the last year, i am still looking forward to it each
morning if it means not talking to you.

olive tostevin

you forced my sister into becoming my protector
at such a young age. my protector from you every
chance she got. *she tried to get your hands off,*
when you shook and pushed me to the floor. you
would call her a bitch so often, shame her for
standing up to you. i know now that bitch just
meant you couldn't tolerate a woman telling you no.
i know she just became everything you weren't for
her, and anything i ever needed her to be. i'll never
see you again and for that i am eternally grateful - *i*
don't want you back anymore. six years without you
has taught me what i deserve. i don't miss you at all,
i hate your heart and your painful mind. wherever
you are, *i hope it's hurting.* the stories my mother
has told of you have me spitting in your absence.
you knew what you were doing. you knew it was
wrong. we are fighting the remnants of you each
and every day, while you are where you belong. i

will get better where you chose to get bitter, i will publish in your name so you are burdened with who you are. if i have to wear this forever i will make sure you do too.

i love who i've become without you here, and i hope god tells you on my behalf.

i won't keep quiet another second - i've carried this with me for long enough.

A note from the author

Thank you for taking the time to read me,
a story of how mental illness, violence against
women, childhood trauma, and my relationship
with God, have all come to affect the way I love
myself. A letter imploring sisters to take care
of their sisters, uplift your female competitors,
choose to empower your daughters. Men have
taken so much from us already, it's time we give
ourselves the love we've always deserved.

Quit that job, move to that country, *write that
book.* What is the purpose if you are doing what
you've always done? We are changing each and
every day, *embrace it,* move with it, listen to your
intuition - it's there for a reason. We are supposed
to be in the forest searching for berries, it doesn't
matter if you make that yellow light. Sit still. Slow
down. Kiss each other, love each other in that
beautiful way men cannot understand.

This page is for my very own veggie patch,
the loves of my life, the friends that became sisters,
the Leahs and Eves.

And to a man named Fish -
I love you Schmuffin. You are heaven on Earth.
But you are absolutely bonkers.

All her love,

Olive x

(The end)